JACKRABBIT
and the PRAIRIE FIRE

The Story of a Black-tailed Jackrabbit

**SMITHSONIAN
WILD HERITAGE COLLECTION**

To Artemis Millan

Printed in Singapore

Library of Congress Cataloging-in-Publication Data

Saunders, Susan.

Jackrabbit and the prairie fire : story of a black-tailed jackrabbit /
written by Susan Saunders ; illustrated by Jo-Ellen Bosson.
                  p.   cm.
Summary: a frightened jackrabbit outruns a hunting coyote and a
fire caused by lightning and finds safety on a river, while rain falls to
extinguish the flames and prevent further destruction.
    ISBN 0-924483-29-6
1. Jackrabbits — juvenile fiction. [1. Prairie ecology — Fiction.
2. Ecology — Fiction.]   I. Bosson, Jo-Ellen, date, ill.   II. Title.
    PZ10.3.S2572 Jac   1991
    [E] — dc20   91-61144
                                        AC

JACKRABBIT
and the PRAIRIE FIRE

The Story of a Black-tailed Jackrabbit

by Susan Saunders

Illustrated by Jo-Ellen Bosson

Soundprints

A Division of Trudy Management Corporation
Norwalk, Connecticut

Jackrabbit is hungry.
Instead of spending the hot
summer afternoon safe in his
shallow resting place under the
sagebrush, he creeps out
onto the prairie.

He pauses, carefully testing his
world for any hints of hidden
dangers. His huge, black-tipped ears
swivel from side to side, gathering in
the tiniest sounds around him.

His nose twitches as he sniffs the air
for the scent of a lurking bobcat, or coyote.
He cocks a nervous brown eye at the sky for
the silent swoop of a red-tailed hawk. Then
he moves cautiously forward. The prairie
grasses sway and rustle around him.

Jackrabbit stops to nibble at a blade or two.
But in the two months since he was born,
it hasn't rained at all. The sun and wind have
burned the grass to a dry, brittle brown.
It falls to pieces in his mouth.

Suddenly there is a scratching noise
from behind a clump of dead weeds nearby.
Jackrabbit freezes.
His ears fold down
against his back.
His large eyes are
unblinking. His coat
blends so well
with the colors
of the prairie
that he is almost
invisible.

But the noise is only a striped ground
squirrel, as hungry as Jackrabbit is,
scratching around for stray weed seeds.
Jackrabbit lopes slowly past him.

As Jackrabbit searches through
the dry grass for food, dark clouds begin
to drift over the sun. Then a flash of
lightning flickers across the sky, followed
by the distant rumble of thunder.

Alarmed, Jackrabbit sits straight up on his hind legs,
his heart pounding, his ears quivering at the troubling
new sound. And the summer storm sweeps toward him.

Cra-ack!
A lightning bolt hurtles downward
to stab the ground. A wisp of gray smoke
appears above the dry grass. It is followed
by a licking flame . . . **Fire!**
The prairie is burning.

One sniff, and Jackrabbit leaps blindly
away, covering ten or fifteen feet of ground
with each giant bound.

He startles a hunting coyote with its nose to the ground. It whirls to chase after him. The coyote cannot catch Jackrabbit, but it forces him farther and farther away from his resting place under the sagebrush.

Just as Jackrabbit is tiring, the prairie grass ends all at once, at the edge of a slow-moving river. He plunges straight into the water, paddling with his front feet.

Jackrabbit pulls himself out on the opposite bank and shakes the water from his fur. He has left the fire behind him, and outrun the hunting coyote.

He is far from his resting place, but there are blades of tender green grass to eat at the river's edge.

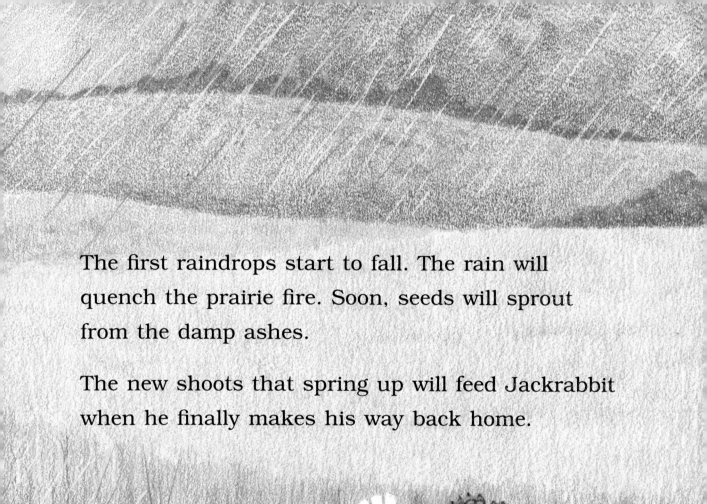

The first raindrops start to fall. The rain will quench the prairie fire. Soon, seeds will sprout from the damp ashes.

The new shoots that spring up will feed Jackrabbit when he finally makes his way back home.

About the Black-tailed Jackrabbit

Living on the open prairies and deserts of the southwestern United States, the black-tailed jackrabbit is one of the fastest members of the rabbit family. It can cover from five to 20 feet per hop and accelerates up to 35 miles per hour over short distances. This jackrabbit, which is actually a hare, is known for its large thin ears, black rump and tail.

Glossary

Bobcat: A common North American wildcat, usually rusty or reddish in color, with a short, stubby tail.

Coyote: A small, dog-like animal found throughout North America, but most numerous on the open plains of the West. Coyotes are best known for their unique howl.

Ground squirrel: A burrowing rodent that lives in colonies, especially in open areas.

Lightning: The flashing of light produced by a discharge of atmospheric electricity from one cloud to another or between a cloud and the earth.

Prairie: Relatively flat grassland with few trees.

Red-tailed hawk: A rodent-eating bird of prey with a short, reddish tail.

Sagebrush: A common North American shrub that often covers large parts of the prairie.

Points of Interest in this Book

p. 13	ladybird beetle
pp. 14–15	a lesson in perspective: the thirteen-lined ground squirrel illustrated in the foreground is actually about one-quarter the size of the more distant jackrabbit shown beyond the bushes.
pp. 16–17	pronghorn
p. 19	western meadowlark
p. 25	coyote
p. 31	fritillary butterfly